I0019497

Thinking of...

Microsoft Office 365 and the Business Conversation?

Ask the Smart Questions

By Frank Bennett & Stephen Parker

Copyright © 2015 Frank Bennett and Stephen Parker

First Published in 2015 by Smart Questions Limited, Fryern House, 125 Winchester Road, Chandlers Ford, Hampshire, SO53 2DR, UK

Web: *www.smart-questions.com* (including ordering of printed and electronic copies, extended book information, community contributions and details on charity donations)

Email: *info@smart-questions.com* (for customer services, bulk order enquiries, reproduction requests et al)

The right of 2015 Frank Bennett and Stephen Parker to be identified as the authors of this book has been asserted in accordance with the Copyright, Designs and Patents Act 1998. All rights reserved. No part of this publication may be reproduced, stored in a retrieval system or transmitted, in any form or by any means, electronic, mechanical, recording or otherwise, in any part of the world, without the prior permission of the publisher. Requests for permission should be sent to the publisher at *info@smart-questions.com*

Designations used by entities to distinguish their products are often claimed as trademarks. All brand names and product names used in this book are trade names, service marks, trademarks or registered trademarks of their respective owners.

The authors and publisher have taken care in preparation of this book, but to the extent permitted by applicable laws make no express or implied warranty of any kind and assume no responsibility for errors or omissions. The contents of this book are general in nature and do not constitute legal or other professional advice. You should always seek specific professional advice relevant to your circumstances. Where specific costs or prices have been given, these represent our best 'standard case' estimates at the time of writing. They are intended to provide a rough indication only and should not be relied on in any way. To the extent permitted by law, no liability is assumed for direct, incidental or consequential loss or damage suffered or incurred in connection with or arising out of the use of the information contained herein.

A catalogue record for this book is available from the British Library.

ISBN 978-1-907453-18-2

SQ-23-189-001-003

Smart Questions™ Philosophy

Smart Questions is built on 4 key pillars, which set it apart from other publishers:

1. *Smart people want Smart Questions not Dumb Answers*
2. *Domain experts are often excluded from authorship, so we are making writing a book simple and painless*
3. *The community has a great deal to contribute to enhance the content*
4. *We donate a percentage of profit to charity. It is great marketing, but it is also the right thing to do*

www.smart-questions.com

Authors

Frank Bennett

Frank has a 30 year career in IT sales & marketing and seen every evolution of computing technology from mainframe to cloud. His insight of how the Internet is shaping commerce and customer buying behaviour has helped many businesses define their go to market strategies. He has published other Smart Questions titles and collaborated with other authors on cloud computing.

frank@frankbennett.co.uk

Stephen Parker

VP Market Research, rhipe Ltd

A business executive and Cloud Computing specialist, with over 25 years' experience of taking business and technology investment decisions and delivering solutions on the leading edge of IT in large enterprises, dotcom start-ups, SMBs, and business turnarounds.

He is now focused on helping businesses maximise their commercial opportunities in the emerging Cloud market.

He has worked closely with leading software vendors on their global cloud strategy, provides associate services to industry analysts, is a keynote speaker and has written a variety of books covering the Cloud space.

stephen@smart-questions.com

Table of Contents

Foreword

In recent times technology has created a social upheaval and as a result we are now dependent of technology to an extent that we have never been before to connect with the world in which we conduct our social life, our work, our learning and amusement.

Today if you want to have a successful business selling IT then you need to accept this social upheaval is influencing the attitudes and choices of consumers and businesses. If you don't, you may end having a conversation that your customer does not recognise. The cloud is familiar vocabulary and the driver of innovation that is landing on the computers, tablets and mobile phones of billions of people and the opportunity expands to new dimensions with the Internet of Things that is fertile for even more innovation. The IT industry is fortunate with abundant opportunity for those that can escape the pull of the past and step into the future to serve up IT 'as a service'.

It is happening now and increasing in velocity as customers turn on 'as a service' for its affordability, convenience and flexibility. This in turn presents opportunity and threat for the IT supply chain, do you jump in or adopt a wait and see approach. It is time to act and then you have many things to consider; your business, your employees, your customers, who you partner with for 'as a service' and what does this all mean for the future. This book will not tell you what to do, rather it will help you navigate the conversation with your colleagues so you make an informed decision as to what is important for your business and its future.

My name is Mitchell Feldman and I am the CEO and Founder of Cloudamour, Microsoft's Worldwide Cloud Partner of the Year 2014 and we offer our customers Office 365, Azure, Managed Services and other Microsoft hosted services. I truly believe that those businesses that grasp this opportunity will prosper in the future and those that don't will find it increasingly challenging to survive. We are bold and we take our customers on a journey to utopia, a world where IT services just work, employees feel empowered and maintenance is pain free. We speak about outcomes for our customers rather than technology as this is the language of 'as a service' and our customers say 'come on in let's talk'.

The best thing about Office 365 and Azure is that the conversations you have with your customers are no longer about technology itself but how you can help them become better businesses using the cloud. The most successful IT companies aren't those with the best skills, but the ones with the greatest vision who can demonstrate their success. Office 365 and Azure help you achieve your vision.

Follow the advice in this book and maybe next year you will be collecting the Microsoft Worldwide Cloud Partner of the Year Award.

I wish you every success.

Mitchell Feldman

CEO and Founder Cloudamour

https://www.cloudamour.com

Who should read this book?

People like you and me

This book was written for Microsoft partners around the world that are looking for opportunities to grow their business 'in the cloud'.

This does not mean an abandonment of all the investment and expertise that you have worked hard to accumulate as a Microsoft partner, rather it is about how you choose to respond to market forces that are changing how IT can be deployed - in the cloud.

Microsoft provide the opportunity with Office 365 to secure a future for your business in the cloud and do so with your existing customers and find new customers.

The book is for everyone in the business as cloud affects every part of your business so please share it around and then everyone can participate in the exercises that we suggest in the book.

If you an owner or shareholder in the business then this book is particularly relevant as it talks about the value of selling Office 365 and that is about your future and the potential value of your business. The book does not suggest that Office 365 is make or break for your business, rather it about how with Office 365 you earn money and create a sustainable business model based on the new economics of serving up IT 'as a service' to your customers.

We know you are busy people and so we have worked hard to be concise as time is of the essence.

How to use this book

This book is intended to be the catalyst for action. We hope that the ideas and examples inspire you to act. So, do whatever you need to do to make this book useful. Use Post-it notes, write on it, rip it apart, or read it quickly in one sitting. Whatever works for you and we hope this becomes your most dog-eared book.

Time for a conversation

Let us congratulate you on being a member of Microsoft's partner ecosystem, you partner with a company that is looking out for your future by investing in cloud computing. It is an exciting time with change and innovation serving up new opportunity and Office 365 is waiting for you to pick it up and run with it. As we explain in the book, Office 365 has a large addressable market and opens the door to opportunity if you want to join in.

The IT industry is perpetually innovating and that can cause consternation for those on the supply and buy side. Your customers are looking for ideas and innovation to help them succeed and you have to deliver or face the prospect of being supplanted. These are challenging times, perhaps even stressful, so in this book we set out to start a conversation to help you make the right decisions for the future of your business - in the cloud.

We both know what it's like to be a Microsoft partner as we created a SaaS application back in 2005 and at that time were pioneering the development of software delivered 'as a service'. It had to work, and we made it work, and through continuous learning and acquired experience we write for the Microsoft community in the Smart Questions series of books.

We are starting a conversation, with you at the centre because only you can decide what is important for your future.

Frank and Stephen

Chapter

1

The Situation

Judge a man by his questions rather than by his answers

Voltaire (French philosopher, 1694 – 1778)

T HE cloud is one of those words that have caused confusion, derision, arguments, laughter and a lot more questions than answers for most people. In this book the authors keep asking questions while bringing common sense and experience to help you make the right decisions for your business. Why do you need to make any decisions? The cloud is part of a new IT agenda for your customers, a new order, and you need to decide if you want to be involved with that conversation, and if you do, what the implications are for your business.

The bottom line is this. The IT industry is undergoing a transformation and it is nothing sinister, it is just progress. It is happening whether you like it or not and the consequence is that you need to decide if you want to play. A visit to Microsoft.com will confirm its commitment to cloud computing and it is using its corporate muscle to accelerate adoption of cloud computing by its partners and customers. While it is not a race there is money to be earned today, so why leave it on the table for someone else? There are businesses growing with Microsoft cloud services. Others are feeling the impact of customers' appetite for cloud and it is happening quicker than they anticipated and their reaction has been swift with office closures and layoffs. You are probably thinking; *we don't want that to happen to us.* So you will want to know what changes if any you need to make to your business and how fast.

We wrote this book to help you create value for your business selling Microsoft Office 365. Intrinsic to that value is an understanding of how that serves your business interests and those of your customers. Your interest is to earn money and that opportunity is linked to how you serve your customers' interest to equip their most important asset - their people - to perform their work. The world of work is changing and technology plays its part; you only need to think about how you went about your work five years or even two years ago and today to know that is true.

Have you created a conversation with your customers to get under their skin so you know how they see the future of IT in their business? In the cloud, technology is submerged and gives way to a conversation about business outcomes and that is perhaps a new conversation for you; particularly when the solution is served up 'as a service' in the cloud. Are you having this conversation?

The cloud serves up the opportunity to reframe the economics of IT (the things you have to afford) and access to innovation (the things you can't always afford and make a difference). This has different implications depending if you are on the supply or demand side.

Money and Cloud Money

What is $50 x 700,000,000? Answer $35,000,000,000.

700,000,000 is a big number and is Gartner's estimate of the numbers of users for cloud office systems by 2022, which multiplied by $50 (a notional price of an annual subscription per user) delivers a prize worth $35Bn annually. That is a recurring revenue stream with near zero cost of sale in year two and beyond. Moreover that is just for the subscription revenue and excludes any professional services. Interested now?

Microsoft Context

Microsoft Key Ambitions[1]
1 billion active Windows 10 devices in FY18
USD20 billion annualised run rate in Commercial Cloud in FY18

[1] Satya Nadella – Microsoft Financial Analyst Briefing – 29th April 2015

With Office 365 Microsoft are making a clear statement that a shift to the cloud is about staying relevant and maintaining the market leading position in a changing IT landscape. Some partners may find the changes involved challenging and disruptive. To put this disruption in context, Office 365's biggest competitor is Microsoft's existing on-premises Office systems solutions, which contributes roughly one-third of Microsoft revenue.

"Do you cannibalise yourself or wait until somebody else does?"

And Office 365 is only one of the growing portfolio of cloud service oriented offerings that Microsoft are bringing to market and in doing so competing with themselves.

Windows 10

With the arrival of Windows 10 it is highly likely that we will also see this 'services' shift extend to the heart of Microsoft's traditional business, the operating system (OS). Microsoft are positioning Windows 10 as the last of the monolithic operating system releases. In future the OS will simply evolve and itself become more like a service. We have already seen this sign posted with Windows Azure as the evergreen platform for Windows Server.

Internet of Things

Bill Gates' famous mantra "A computer on every desk and in every home" was staggering in its scope at the time. The emergence of the Internet of Things is making this seem simply like the entree to the main course. IDC have predicted that by 2020 there will be 212bn devices and an $8.9tn market.

This is impacting Microsoft thinking as was evidenced at WPC 2014 when Satya Nadella discussed how Microsoft were now a "14% market share challenger" in the vastly expanded devices market. We are at the beginning of a huge explosion of opportunity – start a conversation with your customers now and prime them for what will be your next growth opportunity.

Communication and Collaboration

A cloud office system (Gartner's term) is for communication and collaboration, it is how 'we get things done', the everyday and routine tasks and something every business of all size need. The picture turns 'get things done' into a

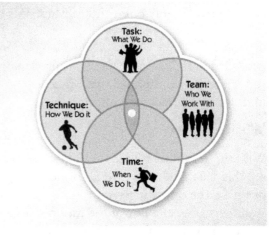

visual image of what happens during the working day, and how these activities are performed can have a big impact on personal and team productivity. Office 365 is in this sweet spot and it is hard to image a business that would not be interested in a conversation that affects the productivity of their workforce. Office 365 is the opportunity to open a conversation your customers are waiting for.

Build Trust

To be the trusted advisor that your customers will turn to when they want to have a conversation about the cloud you will need to decide what is important about that conversation for your customer. What do you think is uppermost in the mind of your customers when they want a conversation about the cloud? Test some assumptions with your customers by leading with open questions that ultimately test the true underlying motivation for their continuing investment in IT. Every business has some level of investment and recurring costs associated with IT and most are open to a conversation that helps them understand and be reassured *they are making the optimal allocation of their resources to deliver the IT for their business.*

That is a conversation you can steer to talk about what the business needs from IT and its current capability to deliver. This is fertile ground to explore where they face constraints, typically money and people, and how they can be overcome with a new approach - in the cloud.

When the conversation turns to money you will need a thorough understanding of the economics of the cloud and its impact on the balance sheet and P&L, as this is something that your customers will expect you to know.

What do the experts say?

IT industry analysts report on the past, the present and make forecasts and predictions about the future. They are all agreed that cloud is here to stay and is transforming the IT industry. Depending which analyst you talk to you will get variations of a common theme.

- IDC talk about 'The Third Platform'
- Gartner talk about 'The Nexus of Forces'

Both position cloud among four trends that include Cloud, Mobile, Social and Big Data. There is a new language for a new era about how IT will be served up and it is happening now.

The conversation about the Cloud is an increasingly mature one. When these conversations include Office 365 they open up the tantalising opportunity of a share of a $35Bn annually recurring spend.

What do customers say?

- The combination of mobile devices and cloud services presents a real opportunity to fundamentally re-think business processes and to alter the way we work.
- Having a progressive end-user computing strategy is an important enabler of business innovation.
- When it comes to end-user computing the business is demanding more than the IT department is currently able to deliver.

- And if you were a fly on the wall: Talk to us about our options for affordable software that boosts productivity in our business.

Talking 'Value'

- Office 365 presents the opportunity to sell a license that generates recurring subscription revenue and that has a value to your P&L. The subscription revenue of Office 365 is not viewed as favourably as the revenue associated with the resale of hardware and software and associated services and that is largely because that has been the underpinning business model of most IT businesses for so long. Lumpy deal-by-deal project revenues that inject cash into the business are replaced by subscription revenues that smooth out cash flow yet take time to accumulate and in the interim create a cash flow hazard. The transition of the business model from project to subscription revenues is a journey that many have completed successfully and come out the other side in stronger financial position but it takes time to complete the transition.

- If you are a shareholder you will have a valuation on your business, the price you would be willing to sell for and that is often different from what a buyer will offer. The value of Office 365 is that its recurring subscription revenues have been demonstrated to enhance the valuation of a business.

- Value is also expressed in terms of your role in a supply chain. As you look upstream and downstream in your supply chain you will have a view of the value of your counterparties. Those that deliver low value are either dispensable or replaced and sometimes that is because their function in the supply chain has been diminished, often by technology. Later in this book we put the question of the value of Office 365 in the supply chain as a tool to enable communication and collaboration that is vital to efficiency of a supply chain. What is your assessment of your value in the supply chain and how do those upstream and downstream view that?

- Perhaps the one that tops them all is the value that your customers put on their relationship with your business as a supplier of IT. Are you seen as conservative or progressive? Sometimes you will mirror your customer; 'We are a progressive business and prefer to deal with suppliers that share our stance'. Whatever your stance the rate of innovation means that your customers may miss out as the cloud increasingly levels the IT playing field and they won't thank you for that. Do not let them or you get left behind.

The opportunity is there for the taking.

Just one more thing

Do nothing is always an option. However consider the scenario that more and more IT will be consumed 'as a service' and that Microsoft will continue to develop software for delivery 'as a service'. It is easy to get left behind but there is no reason for that and selling Office 365 gets you in the game. Check out the Microsoft Cloud Solution Provider (CSP) program to see how Microsoft is evolving.

https://mspartner.microsoft.com/en/us/pages/solutions/cloud-reseller-overview.aspx

Chapter

2

The Complications

"Where there is a will there is a way"

Samuel Smiles (Author and Government reformer, 1812 - 1904)

YOU have probably heard the expression 'you don't know what you don't know'. The truth is that while many people happily use cloud in their vocabulary, when pushed to explain what it is they are lost for words. This is as true for those that work in the IT industry as those that don't. So one of the complications for anyone selling cloud services is that you will meet a lot of people who will nod when you say the word cloud but have not a clue what you are talking about. Perhaps the motto is: never assume the person you are talking to knows' what the cloud is. The key is to talk to your customer in their language about their business issues and then introduce the cloud as a solution. Here is one way to think and talk about the cloud - *new opportunities.*

Beware the answer

Do you use cloud services? No, hang on, I'm not sure, perhaps we do or maybe we don't.

Depending who you ask in an organisation you may get inconsistent answers to this question. Here are a few reasons why few people can honestly answer this question:

1. Employees are using cloud services on personal devices that can access corporate data but there is no way to know that without asking employees.

2. LOB managers sanction the cost out of local budgets and provided the access to the cloud service provider is not blocked (by corporate firewall) then who is the wiser.
3. Apps for cloud services on mobile phones and tablets that are not tethered to corporate networks and are rarely subject to the security controls of PCs.

So, in a world of so much confusion and the cloud being delivered outside of the traditional IT team ('Stealth Cloud') who do you talk to?

Watch your back

The size of the prize has been the catalyst for 'born in the cloud' businesses and these businesses are out to steal your customers and pose a different threat to the competitors you are familiar with. Hey, don't worry, you have customers and they are loyal to you, aren't they? So what are you

> Born in the Cloud. A term used for businesses that have started up only to sell cloud services. With no customer legacy their sales tactics are different and as an unproven supplier need to approach the customer as a problem solver and of course, cloud is always the answer.

going to say to them about this new fangled cloud computing thing and why they should consider Office 365?

Microsoft has announced that Office 365 is its fastest growing business of all time and Gartner (as well as other analysts) have strong growth forecasts for the Cloud. However your ability to build a profitable business around Office 365 will depend on qualifying your existing customers and the potential to acquire new customers. It is also highly dependent on your willingness to embrace change. Your move.

Low hanging fruit

Organisations depend on communication and collaboration to deliver productivity and 'get work done' efficiently and you don't have to look far for opportunity as every organisation has this requirement – *it satisfies a known demand and every customer that use the Microsoft Office suite is a prospect.*

Low hanging fruit attracts a lot of interest; so what is your differentiating value proposition that will send the competition packing?

You will have to look inside your business to understand what your core competencies and skills are so you remain the preferred partner for your customer. What are these skills, what is the value to the customer and how does this impact the way you are setup today to best serve your customers?

These are potential complications that will disrupt how you are currently setup to win business and deliver projects. For example, has your sales approach been technically led or a more consultative approach teasing out the business challenges and then solving with a technology solution?

Choices

If you are packing up in 3 - 5 years and switching the lights off for the last time then you can probably ignore the cloud, but expect things to get more challenging as you compete for business against those that do offer cloud services. If your horizon is beyond 3 - 5 years then waste no time building a recurring revenue stream. It is widely reported that businesses relying primarily on resale of hardware are experiencing margins being squeezed (some say, out of existence). On the other hand services are seen as resilient source of revenue and profit particularly those that generate recurring revenue such as Office 365.

Transitioning from resale to a business model that is tuned to delivery of cloud services can take 2 - 3 years before the cumulative effect of recurring revenues underpin profitability. That said, the transition is progressive and does not mean a complete exit from a resale model, rather reduced dependency on resale and increased dependency on recurring revenue. It is a bet, your bet that customers will shun or favour deployment of IT 'as a service' although heed the evidence. The watchword here is don't be complacent, this is a high growth market and competitors like those born in the cloud prey on complacency.

Another choice is the bet that IT 'as a service' is the future and of course you will want to test that with your customers. Even if they are not ready you will have seized the initiative and if they are ready then you have a potential sale.

With so many choices for both you and your customers the biggest complication may be your indecision?

We end this chapter with a quotation: The person who gets the farthest is generally the one who is willing to do and dare. The 'sure-thing' boat never gets far from shore. *Dale Carnegie, author of "How to Win Friends and Influence People"*

Chapter

Ask the Smart Questions

If I have seen further it is by standing on the shoulders of giants

Isaac Newton (Scientist, 1643 – 1727)

SMART Questions is about giving you valuable insights or "the Smarts". Normally these are only gained through years of painful and costly experience. Whether you already have a general understanding of the subject and need to take it to the next level or are starting from scratch, you need to make sure you ask the Smart Questions. We aim to short-circuit that learning process, by providing the expertise of the 'giants' that Isaac Newton referred to.

Not all the questions will necessarily be new or staggeringly insightful. The value you get from the information will clearly vary. It depends on your job role and previous experience. We call this the 3Rs.

The 3 Rs

Some of the questions will be in areas where you know the answers already so the book will **Reinforce** them in your mind.

You may have forgotten some aspects of the subject, so the book will **Remind** you.

Other questions may **Reveal** new insights to you that you've never considered before.

How do you use Smart Questions?

The questions are laid out in a series of structured and ordered tables with the questions in one column and the explanation of why it matters alongside. We've also provided a checkbox so that you can mark which questions are relevant to your particular situation.

A quick scan down the first column in the list of questions should give you a general feel of where you are for each question vs. the 3Rs. At the highest level they are a sanity check or checklist of areas to consider.

We trust that you will find real insights. There may be some "aha" moments. Hopefully not too many sickening, head in the hands "what have we done' moments. Even if you do find yourself in such a situation, the questions may help you to re-establish some order, take control and steer you back into calmer waters.

In this context, probably the most critical role of the Smart Questions is to reveal risks that you might not have considered. On the flip side they should also open up your thinking to opportunities that hadn't yet occurred to you. Balancing the opportunities and the risks, and then agreeing what is realistically achievable is the key to formulating an effective strategy.

And finally

Please remember that these questions are NOT intended to be a prescriptive list that must be followed slavishly from beginning to end. It is also inevitable that the list of questions is not exhaustive and we are confident that with the help of the community the list of Smart Questions will grow.

If you want to rephrase a question to improve its context or have identified a question we've missed, then let us know to add to the collective knowledge.

We also understand that not all of the questions will apply to all businesses. However we encourage you to read them all, as there may be a nugget of truth that can be adapted to your circumstances.

Above all we do hope that it provides a guide or a pointer to the areas that may be valuable to you and helps with the "3 Rs".

Chapter

The Storyboard

I like the dreams of the future better than the history of the past.

Thomas Jefferson (3rd president of US, 1743 - 1826)

THERE are many ways to construct a story and start a conversation with your customer about Office 365. In this chapter we look to the background to what is happening with the pervasive use of the Internet and increasing adoption of cloud computing and services like Office 365 and how that is shaping conversations between Microsoft partners and customers. Customer first. Later in the book we turn to matters important to your business.

Keep in mind

The simplicity of Office 365 is that it offers tangible customer benefits.

1. **Cash flow**. Monthly fees are predictable and set against operating expenditure budgets rather than capital expenditure to deliver a healthier balance sheet.
2. **Availability**. Financially backed Service Level Agreements provide assurances for the availability of the service.
3. **Access**. Anywhere there is an Internet connection.
4. **Convenience**. Get on with your business while Microsoft and you take care of the 'IT'.
5. **Advantage**. Affordable access to software that boosts productivity in your business.

We could almost end this chapter here if you took nothing else away than memorising the benefits of Office 365. However the purpose of the chapter is to put in context what is driving the appetite to rethink the deployment of IT in the cloud and use cloud services like Office 365.

Core to conversations with your customers is explaining the choice that customers now have to deploy IT. For many customers this is a new conversation and permits you to explore many different aspects related to their vision of IT, and of course you can help them define that.

IT transformation driven by need to reduce costs and look at alternatives

- Legacy IT
- Build to order
- Slow to deploy
- Own & Operate

Slower!

£ £ £

CAPEX and people intensive

- Cloud / Web enabled
- Configure to order
- Fast to deploy
- Services culture

Faster!

OPEX and collaborative with partners

That can include the financial alternatives of CAPEX versus OPEX and other costs to include personnel, real estate, energy and pursuit of their 'green' agenda. *This could be a defining moment for your future with a customer as you help them create a future vision for IT.*

Markets are Conversations

What conversations are informing the market (think customers) and are you part of that conversation? Can you help interpret the noise of a highly vocal IT industry and piece together the jigsaw puzzle of statistics and surveys and sometimes hype for your customers? Here are some we have found (current at time of publication of this book).

- 88% of UK IT Directors believe that an end-user computing strategy is an important enabler of business innovation. *You can enter this conversation with Office 365.*

- A survey of 800 companies by Colt across eight European countries highlighted a 'technology deficit' and specifically identified voice and communications (88 per cent), data centre infrastructure (90 per cent) and network infrastructure (85 per cent) as key areas for improvement. One more thing, and every IT supplier should take not of this: the research unearths a trend to more consolidation of suppliers and strategic partners, with 63 per cent of respondents stating they see benefit in a single supplier model that provides a range of different IT service and infrastructure options. *Step up to the plate with the Microsoft Cloud Solution Provider program.*

- The combination of mobile devices and cloud services presents a real opportunity to fundamentally re-think business processes, and to alter the way work gets done. In addition, communication and collaboration can be extended well beyond the traditional desk-based employee and the corporate network. *You can enter this conversation with Office 365.*

- According to IDC: SaaS delivery will significantly outpace traditional software product delivery growing nearly five times faster than the software market as a whole and by 2018 the cloud software model will account for $1 of every $5 spent on software. *Put that in the context of your own customers and what that would mean for their spend and importantly your sales.*

The bottom line is that the world is perpetually in a state of flux and there is always opportunity as highlighted above and balanced out by practical considerations. What most customers want to know is; *are they spending their hard-earned cash on IT that is optimised for their business to help make them successful, and one more thing, is affordable?* They are looking to you to help them answer that question.

The customer point of view

- Is there a way I can wind back the complexity of IT and with it the cost?

- Here is our list of wants: Simplification, Flexibility, and Efficiency. How do I get there?
- I need to introduce flexible working arrangements for my staff and to attract new talent. How can technology help?
- I think I am taking all necessary precautions to keep my data safe. I often wonder; is there another way, a better way?
- IT can be baffling. I would really like 'cards on the table' and put my business at the heart of the conversation about IT. I'm happy in the knowledge: I win, You win.
- There are just so many choices, this one, that one, help me choose wisely for my business. Tell me why it is a wise decision and what the future looks like with that decision made.
- Is more for less possible? That would be different to the usual; 'that is going to cost you' conversation with my IT supplier.
- I leave my computer in the office these days and go about with my smartphone and sometimes a tablet. It is more convenient and if this becomes the way we all work then what is the IT we need to support this freedom? Is that the cloud?
- What are the trade-offs putting our IT in the cloud versus continuing with 'own and operate'? And can I mix both?
- What is happening in my supply chain; are others using cloud computing?
- If I use cloud computing will that help my business to win more customers?
- More and more of our transactions are being delivered through the cloud. Is it the same for other businesses? What are they doing about that?
- I have no experience specifying and buying cloud services. Who do I trust?

These points may be modified according to whether you are in conversation with a global corporation or a small business and they deal with the tensions between how the IT industry talks about IT and what is on the mind of customers. They are not really interested that V12.0 is on schedule for release unless it is the resolution to a bug that is harming their business.

How about this as a motto for all your customers' conversations: *Let's talk about IT as part of the future rather than part of the furniture.*

Crowdbraining

A made up word but topical to the way in which we now enrich how we work. Bring your team together, sales, marketing, finance, admin, everyone's views count and crowdbrain these two questions:

1.   With the cloud we can..
2.   With the cloud our customers can..

Let the ideas flow and see what happens as this is essential preparation for those all important customer conversations.

Move it on and substitute the word 'cloud' for 'Office 365' in the two questions. If you do not have much experience with Office 365 then read the book 'Thinking of...Selling Office 365? Ask the Smart Questions' by the authors of this book. This is available to download for free from Microsoft Partner Network.

Qualify your customer

Next we turn our attention to tuning a conversation for your customers that helps you to qualify their interest in Office 365.

Cost reduction

Their interest is to drive cost out of the business and only those initiatives that deliver a quick ROI, lower TCO or deliver on the bar set for a NPV calculation get considered. This customer is looking at low risk - high return and you need to set the expectation early during the first sales call to gain their attention. A potential quick win for you if the numbers add up for your customer.

Desire innovation

Perhaps they have more appetite for risk and are willing to consider new and innovative approaches to deliver on productivity or improve how they serve customers. A more thoughtful approach to how technology can be applied to people and processes but more work for you to qualify how strong that appetite is and discover where the challenges are in the business. Potentially a longer sales cycle but with the upside of professional services revenue from consulting and development attaching to implementation, training and support/managed service.

You may instantly recognise that you associate with one of these two scenarios more than the other and that may be a condition of your current value proposition and/or skills and experience. Have you qualified your customers to know which of the two scenarios applies?

Risk vs. Reward Scenarios

Another view on your customers pivots around their motivation in relation to risk and reward:

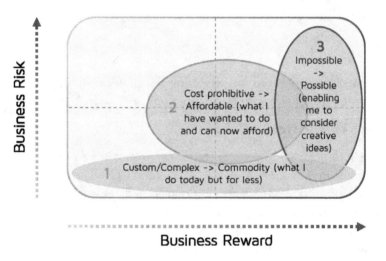

Type 1: For some motivation is driven primarily by cost reduction. This is a natural starting point. Your opportunity even within this area is to help the customer increase their business reward, without increasing risk. An example of this could be the deployment Office

365 to reduce headline costs and then driving value by adding basic business workflows within SharePoint.

Type 2: The cloud may be an opportunity to revisit ideas that have been previously rejected due to costs and complexity. Can Office 365 change the economics of IT enabling franchise operations or remote offices? Can you now enable all staff to have sophisticated collaboration tools and not just the desk bound office workers and in doing so make radical changes to existing processes?

Type 3: Through delivering on the Type 1 & 2 motivations you may earn the right to work with your customer on imagining the impossible. 'If this were now possible, what previously fanciful ideas could we now consider?'

The call you are not waiting for

What if your customers called you into a meeting and said: we are not spending any more money on IT until we have a 'vision' for how that is going to serve the business and deliver more value than we feel we are getting today. Can you help? Your inclination will probably be to say Yes, after all the cost of sale to acquire a new customer is high compared to the costs of serving an existing customer. So now you have to imagine the conversation that your customers expect of you. If you had to answer this question here and now: Does your 'vision' include the cloud? Yes or No.

In the following chapter we suggest some questions to engage your customers in conversation to expose your sales opportunity.

Chapter

10 Questions to ask your customers

Laughter gives us distance. It allows us to step back from an event, deal with it and then move on.

Bob Newhart (Comedian, 1929 –)

IT took 75 years for telephones to be used by 50 million customers, but it took only four years for the Internet to reach that many users. Those in hi-tech businesses know all about change and how rapidly change can make or break a business.

Perhaps your customers are already using cloud services – *do you know that?*

This section is about putting your feet in the shoes of your customers and opening up to possibilities that might sway your customers: we know why we have to invest in IT but if we have the choice to own and operate (on-premises) or pay a subscription for cloud services - which would be better for our business and why?

☒	Question	Why this matters
☐	5.1.1 Do you offer your customers' service contracts?	The services industry is vast and accounts for >60% of global GDP. It is a fair chance that your customers offer services to their customers. Explore with them what the benefits are to their customers. Why do this? Office 365 is offered as a service on terms that will be understood by your customers if they offer services. People are much more likely to buy what they understand. Be ready to talk about the benefits customers see from IT delivered as a service. Explain that this is the future of IT and you would like your customer's permission to keep them updated about options that you consider would be of benefit to their business. Be bold and propose a joint planning meeting with a 1-hour time limit to expose what IT 'as a service' might deliver for their business.
☐	5.1.2 Are you getting requests from your employees for flexible working arrangements?	Technology is an enabler and you need to ask the right questions to expose what is on your customer's mind, and sometimes, what they have not thought about. Customers value suppliers that bring new insights to their business with practical solutions. Retaining talent and finding new talent is often cited as a challenge faced by employers. Talking through solutions that give them options to deal with important matters can lead to opportunity for you.

☒	Question	Why this matters
☐	5.1.3 Is your IT delivering the quality of service that you need to support your business?	This is a provocative question and a different way to approach a conversation. It may be met with; define quality of service. This is the reason to ask the question in the first place. Customers are unlikely to spend money they don't need to, in the case that the quality of service of existing IT is satisfactory. Where it is not there is opportunity. What IT is not delivering the quality of service required by the business? What are the alternatives? People at the decision table think in terms of what they are trying to achieve, such as improving customer satisfaction leading to more repeat orders and referrals. How they achieve that is not always so obvious and may be a factor that IT is not delivering the quality of service to support what they strive to achieve.
☐	5.1.4 Do you know the true cost of providing your employees email and other must have tools to perform their work?	Most will say No or guess. In many ways this goes to the rationale of IT 'as a service' as you and they will know exactly what it costs. Your customer has 50 employees all requiring email. You can price that with Office 365 and do that for the next 3 years so you can show the benefit of having a known cost to the business. Don't trouble your customer with what their current costs are they usually don't know so show the cost of standing up the same services on-premises (to include disaster recovery) and the resulting cash flow implications.

☒	Question	Why this matters
☐	5.1.5 How do you manage compliance with software license T&Cs? Would you prefer to remove this burden and worry? Do you find it easy to accurately budget for changes to the number of users?	No one likes talking about compliance as it often exposes weaknesses. Customers will be interested however in three things: 1. They are compliant with software licensing T&Cs. All licenses are legal. 2. Their usage of software is optimal for the number of users. That is, they only pay for what they need. 3. They can easily and accurately budget for an increase or decrease in the number of users. All of these points are addressed when a customer chooses to use Office 365.
☐	5.1.6 Do you have a plan for BCDR? (Business Continuity & Disaster Recovery)	Customers rarely have a reliable plan for BCDR and the common reasons are: 1. Hope - It won't happen to us. 2. Cost - It is unaffordable. 3. Expertise - It is complex. 4. Tomorrow - It is a tomorrow 'to do' but never is. A customer can relax and get on with their business as Office 365 removes all these worries and BCDR is included in the price of the subscription.
☐	5.1.7 Do you work with contractors and freelancers and need them to use your processes?	Modern businesses look for ways to scale using contractors and freelancers yet need them to be integrated into their processes. The cost of provisioning software to on-board them can be prohibitive and particularly so when the contract is short-term. Microsoft subscription terms for Office 365 offer choices to match function/cost/time to the needs of dynamic resourcing.

☒	Question	Why this matters
☐	5.1.8 What sources of information do your customers rely upon for research?	Enterprise customers have the resources to conduct research and employ consultants to advise them and earlier in the book we quoted Gartner and IDC. Most businesses (SME/SMB) rely on an industry trade body or government sponsored research and you should know what research is available that is informing them about IT and new developments such as the cloud.
☐	5.1.9 Have you a forward in time projection of your IT costs?	Many customers base their budget assumption that next year's cost will be an increase on the current year. Without alternative options this is a safe assumption. By asking the question you invite the opportunity to present alternatives. Break the mould!
☐	5.1.10 What are the trends in your industry and how do you know which to follow and which to ignore?	This question reveals the appetite of a customer to first acknowledge that trends exist and also how they treat them. 'We are not a first mover we tend to wait to the last minute, versus, we look into new trends to see what they offer and act accordingly.' Judge how they answer the question, as it will help you to understand their propensity for change. It will also offer clues for you to understand how to proceed with your sale.

There is plenty of experience with cloud computing and Office 365 and stories found at *www.microsoft.com* to add spice to your customer conversations.

Chapter

6

Baseline the conversation

Change is the essence of life

Reinhold Niebuhr (American theologian, 1892 - 1971)

T HERE are many sources of information that offer projections for growth of cloud and they are constantly revised, generally upward, only you can decide if this information is relevant to you. Perhaps more useful is insight to what really matters for your business.

So what does matter to your business?

Self-examination

Just as you are thinking about your future and cloud because it is topical and fast becoming mainstream, so are your customers and they look to someone to have that conversation with. This should be thrown in the mix of things that baseline the conversation that we now develop.

It is prudent to make the assumption that your customers are interested in having a conversation about the cloud. That may turn out to be wise because you then grab the conversation before someone else takes that initiative.

Ask yourself; if I were in my customers' position to whom would I turn to? Hopefully they will turn to you, the people who have supplied IT to the business before and someone they have a trusted relationship with. With your knowledge of their existing IT investments and with their best interest at heart you should be well positioned to develop their interest in the cloud and convert that into your sales opportunity.

Customer surveys reveal the top motivations of customers to implement cloud services like Office 365 are:

- Improved business agility
- Speed of deployment
- Lower overall costs
- To plug their own IT skill shortages
- Switch IT costs from CAPEX to OPEX
- Reallocation of lean resources to priority projects

Satisfying the needs of your customer must be a priority. However this still needs to happen within the context of the vision, motivations and goals of your business.

That list calls out the things that you will want to understand for your business:

- Your cash flow and P&L
- Customer acquisition strategy
- Sales and support processes
- Impact on project services revenues
- Scope for development of IP
- Creation of new services
- The skill set of your work force
- Account Management
- Consequence to the valuation of the business

This list is neither exhaustive nor entirely specific to Office 365, rather a result of changes that are taking place anyway, as your suppliers and customers embrace the cloud.

Indulge your customer

Start thinking about how you will open a new conversation with your customers where perhaps you deliberately choose not to use the word 'cloud', rather you use open questions in the style of:

- How do you plan and budget for IT?
- How would you like/expect to change that?

- When you think about IT what are your thoughts about; what you would like more of, and for that matter, what you would like less of?

This is business as usual, sitting down with customers and understanding their needs and requirements and dispensing the best advice. Today that conversation has to include the cloud.

Assess the implications

The popular view is that the cloud is changing how IT is consumed and the implications of that are big. That should not be a reason to be 'paralyzed by analysis' rather it is a 'time for decisive action'.

To engage the mind for decisive action, consider this: if today you were starting up a new business to sell IT would your business model include the cloud? Yes or No.

Of course it is easy to talk about change however it is not always easy. In fact it is highly likely that if change seems easy then you have probably missed something! Understanding that change has steps backwards as well as forwards is key to the business transformation process. One model that describes the challenges associated with change is the "Transtheoretical model" from James Prochaska and Carlo Di Clemente.

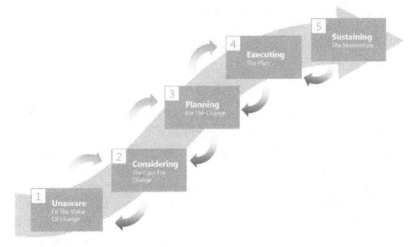

Key messages from their research are that:

Whether individuals or organizations, change is not a one-step, but rather a multi-step process.

These steps occur at different rates for different people.

- Based on the experience or degree of success at a particular stage, a person or organization may return to a previous stage in the change process.
- In order to change and advance through the various stages, individuals must make a conscious decision to modify their thinking and behaviour.
- Research has indicated that self-imposed change is the only effective means for achieving long-term, stable results.

Many Microsoft partners have made the journey to cloud and fortunately the experience of those partners has been captured in a recently completed research project. The conclusions of that research are:

- Not all partners are the same, so integrating Office 365 into their business models will vary—but can be done successfully across these business types

- Partners that do resell Office 365 can boost their operating margins, compared to delivering equivalent premise offerings or other cloud services

- Some partners are successfully accelerating the sales process for Office 365 and other cloud services, cutting the sales time in half compared to using traditional, premise-oriented sales processes

---

More detailed information about the transition and growth path for VARs and SIs moving to offer cloud services can be read in a book by the same authors. See Bibliography.

The future is in your hands

Start to develop a storyline around IT 'as a service' and link to this to a future vision of IT for your customers' business. This does not have to be a distant future it just has to be vision where you help customers make a value judgement about the prioritisation of investment they make in IT. These are not purely technical judgements they interlace with the business outcome. For example, an application that must be available 24/7 and under the control of the customer because in their opinion the data is so commercially sensitive they are not yet ready to consider any alternative to 'in-house', is a quality of service statement. In this case they will pay whatever is required for that quality of service because of its importance. Develop a quality of service matrix where you and your customer populate the matrix to identify opportunity areas and develop a vision.

Here is an example:

Task	Quality of Service	Current Situation	Preferred Situation
Document creation	Must be available 24/7 Access from anywhere and any device Automated version control Secure - easy to control access rights Able to share with external collaborators and control privileges Work with any browser Consistent use of brand and style sheets	Documents scattered over personal devices make version control a nightmare Documents attached to email means no control over distribution Brand and style sheets not being used consistently Issues with external collaborators caused by software incompatibility No BCDR plan - let's hope we never need it! No register of software assets. Are we over/under licensed? Are we legal?	One source of the truth - elimination of version control issues Compliance - control over who has copies of important documents - no more attaching documents to email On/Off access for external collaborators Work from any device anywhere An end to the worry of having no BCDR plan. Control over software assets and cost optimised for usage.

With your knowledge of Office 365 work through the current and preferred situation to create a win - win for your customer.

Seller or Solver?

How many of your customers are you the sole supplier of IT? Do you simply engage with your customers when there is procurement or do you understand their business and help solve business challenges and expose the economic choices to do that? Is the cloud one of the options you are confident to present to your customer?

'Customers put the highest value on salespeople who make them think, who bring new ideas, who find creative and innovative ways to help the customer's business.' In recent years customers have been demanding more depth and expertise. They expect salespeople to teach them things they don't know.'

Quoted from 'The Challenger Sale' by Matthew Dixon and Brent Adamson and a worthwhile read.

Those that are selling cloud services like Microsoft Office 365 acknowledge that the conversation is topical to the CxO team and they are not interested in technobabble. In Chapter 4 we suggested an exercise to prepare you for the CxO conversation.

Overall Strategy

Research by rhipe (an APAC Cloud distributor) found that successful cloud partners have four areas of their overall strategy.

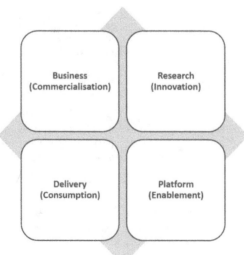

1. Research – this is the engine of innovation that helps maintain differentiation
2. Platform – the choices of tools and solutions that enable you to meet the customer needs
3. Delivery – making the consumption of your services 'friction free' for you customer
4. Business – ensuring that you can profitably commercialise your services

The rhipe research also showed that partners with a technical background had strong Research and Platform strategies but less well developed Delivery and Business strategies. The opposite was true for partners with a strong sales-led culture.

Choices are yours

Build, Resell or Refer. Do you choose 1, 2 or all 3 for your go-to-market? Given your existing customers are most accessible you will certainly want to assess the opportunity with them and you cannot do that without opening up a conversation about cloud. To a large degree your choices will be a factor of where you are starting out from and where you see your future as a supplier of IT and that may redefine your role. Cloud is a game changer and those that have been in a business and witnessed the failure of businesses at the top of their game will know that success is perishable. This is a timely place to remind you about the Microsoft Cloud Solution Provider (CSP) program.

Same team or new team?

So you think you want to sell cloud services and now need to know if you create a new team to go-to-market or go with the existing team. Only you will know the answer to this question! This book does not address this important point so we direct you to you a book with the title 'Escape Velocity' by Geoffrey Moore of 'Crossing the Chasm' fame.

Understanding the Bow Tie Diagram

The shift to the cloud model is much more than just technology it talks to business transformation.

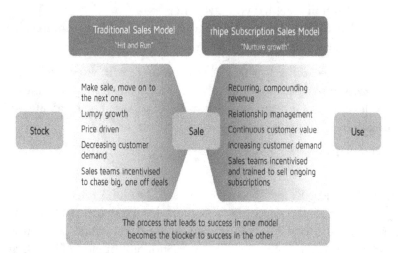

Left side of the bow tie

There is a fundamental change in where the risk lies. Historically it has been a buyer beware world where the risk transfers from the seller to the buyer at the point of the sales transaction. The skills and processes on the left side of the bow tie are designed to convince everyone of the ability to deliver on the "promised value".

Right side of the bow tie

In the world of cloud economics the first sales transaction is only the beginning. With due diligence completed the real proof is provided by the realisation of value as the service is used. If the seller has over-promised and the value is not realised then the customer can exit and stop paying. This is now a seller beware world and proactive customer engagement leading to ongoing use are critical.

The processes that make companies great on the left side of the bow tie can become inhibitors in their transformation to the right side and so it should be recognized that *past success is no guarantee of future success.*

Focus Areas

A wordle of the text of this chapter follows to remind the focus for baseline the conversation and because they are pretty to look at.

Baseline the conversation

Chapter

7

10 Questions for you

Sometimes the questions are complicated and the answers are simple

Dr Seuss US author & illustrator (1904 - 1991)

SOME fear the cloud because it challenges the money earned from an existing business model that has to-date served the business well. Money is money however it is earned and if your business is looking for growth then the cloud is the place to look for growth.

The upset for some is that traditional revenue streams are challenged as the cloud puts more focus on the delivery of services and less on the sale of hardware and software. If services are your primary business activity then the cloud is heaven-sent – you are all set. If services are an adjunct to your operations or have a dependency on the sale of hardware and software then you have to consider how to model your business to offer both.

Keep in mind that as customers look into the cloud, and the evidence is that interest and adoption is fast increasing, then your business needs to evolve depending on how you view the opportunity. Office 365 is priced to attract customers and every partner can sell Office 365 and decide what services to wraparound to earn money.

You can start selling Office 365 today or any time you are ready but keep in mind that the sooner you start the sooner you start the accumulation of a recurring revenue stream.

☐	Question	Why this matters
☐	7.1.1 Do you understand the differences between selling a project and cloud service like Office 365?	There are some similarities in that your project services may overlap those required with the delivery and support of Office 365. The difference with cloud services is the focus on customer retention to ensure the renewal of their subscription to the service being the on-going source of revenue and profit that makes these services so attractive. With a project you can receive feedback during and upon completion of the project and the job is done. With cloud services you have to routinely monitor customers' the use of services and satisfaction. This actually has the benefit of keeping you close to your customer and through that dialogue look for further opportunities that don't present so easily when you walk off-site after delivering a project. What methods do you have in place to measure customer satisfaction and take corrective measures when highlighted?

☐	Question	Why this matters
☐	7.1.2 Do you know who the Top 5 suppliers are to your customers? If not, ask!	Your customers' supply chain is vital to the success of their business. Those suppliers may also be your customers or suppliers to another of your customers. Customers value suppliers that understand the importance of their supply chain and the role of technology to deliver efficiency and lower costs. Office 365 supports efficient communication and collaboration and that is something every business needs. So how can you help and show your customers ways to deliver efficiency and lower costs as a participant in their supply chain. This may seem a small thing but the impact for you as a supplier in the eyes of your customer is much bigger. Don't just think in terms of how you serve your customer but also your customers' upstream and downstream supply chain.
☐	7.1.3 What is your innovation agenda?	Earlier we referred to qualifying your customers' motivation either as cost reduction or desire for innovation. Cost reduction is quantifiable and many can perform that financial calculation including a customer. Innovation relies on creativity and is sought after but also elusive. The cloud is transforming strategic resources like IT into commodity and is a cost of business but does not provide any particular distinction. Innovation is the way to differentiate your proposition and is the 'value' a customer places on dealing with you rather than anyone else. In Chapter 4 we refer to exercises involving all your team to develop your innovation agenda.

☐	Question	Why this matters
☐	7.1.4 Have you completed scenario plans where the assumption is all of your Office customers move to Office 365 over time?	This is not a dare to scenario rather a constructive exercise to understand the implications for your sales forward in time. If you moved every customer to Office 365 in the next 1 to 3 years what would be the implications? For that matter if they moved with another supplier what be the consequences?
☐	7.1.5 Have you explored ways for you and your customers to exchange and collaborate on business documents using Office 365?	If you are a supplier then you will be exchanging documents with your customers. How do you do this and have you considered if there is a better way? You are part of a supply chain and it is incumbent upon every participant in a supply chain to drive efficiency and reduce waste. It seems a simple idea but the world is now digital and your customers look to you to help them understand how to conduct their business in a digital world. Then help them replicate upstream and downstream in their supply chain.
☐	7.1.6 Have you mapped your sales and support processes?	If you sell hardware and software and associated services you will know your sales and support processes and associated cost of customer acquisition and how to make a profit on a sale. Have you mapped these for sales of Office 365 to existing customers and for net new customers? The differences in the timing of revenue and impact on cash flow and profit need to be examined.

☐	Question	Why this matters
☐	7.1.7 Is everyone on-board?	In the book we put the question: same team or new team? Not everyone in the business may have the same enthusiasm or optimism for selling cloud services and Office 365. You can ask everyone but not get a straight answer. Running the exercise in Chapter 4 will help expose the sentiment and enthusiasm of participants. What does that reveal?
☐	7.1.8 Do you know what your customers' industry or trade body is reporting as top challenges for the sector and are you using that information to inform your conversations?	Great news, you can find this out quickly with a search in Bing. It is a fair bet that some of those challenges will have a technology perspective and today that means 'online'. You may not be as expert as your customer in their sector yet you bring new perspectives and that is a mark of value in your customer's eyes. Don't make this too high brow until you have established credibility; bold statements like a goal for 'zero inefficiency' will likely be met with dismay. Lessons from top performing sports teams include looking for incremental improvements over a number of connected processes rather than a 50% improvement in any one that is a big ask and likely to fail. Communication and collaboration is something that every business strives to excel at and there are many opportunities in the myriad of processes to find those improvements. Office 365 is the platform to deliver communication and collaboration.

☐	Question	Why this matters
☐	7.1.9 Have you set up your customers to ambush your competitors?	Prepare your customers for when (and they almost certainly will) receive calls from prospective suppliers offering cloud services and some of those may be competitive to Office 365. Think about what matters to your customers and the reliance they have on IT. The cloud is still novel and competitive suppliers will use this to enter a conversation with your customers. It is your duty to protect your business with your customers and protect them from unwittingly succumbing to sharp talk 'that the cloud is going to save them a ton of money'. It may do, but you want to hold that conversation so seize the initiative before someone else does.
☐	7.1.10 Sales of Office 365 have overtaken Office. Do your customers know this?	This is a 'so what' statement. Yes and it also evidences a trend that your customers may not know about. Turn this into a story: "Sales of Office 365 have overtaken Office and I've been studying why that is. There are good reasons and what I would like to propose with your permission is to explore if those reasons would benefit your business?" Everything before provides the ammunition for this conversation. One more thing; what is it that you cannot reliably predict? The future. It is to an extent out of your control and a reason for the success of Office 365 is the flexibility it offers customers in an uncertain world and this is true for all IT delivered 'as a service'. It is the way it is and customers are receptive so you are pushing on an open door.

As you consider the questions above you probably have front of mind questions about the sales process for Office 365. There will be questions that you need to ask of customers and you will find some examples in the following chapter. That still leaves open the question about the sales process, how you identify a prospect, qualify their interest and deliver a winning proposal. It is not the intention to teach you how to sell, rather to inspire you to use your experience and of course your knowledge of your customers to develop a way to move a conversation from expression of interest to a sale.

Every business has to make a profit and an understanding of how that profit is generated is vital. The experience of partners selling Office 365 is that every $1 of subscription fees can generate $7 in services revenue. For many this comes as a surprise because Office 365 does not require many of the services customarily associated with the supply of hardware and software. So, how are the services revenue generated? This question is answered in a book by the same authors, see Bibliography.

As for the sales process, those in sales look to identify a compelling event so you need to know if your customer has a compelling event that is the driver for action. Sometimes this is a matter of timing with a financial year end, budget planning cycle, IT refresh, IT failure, new CxO appointment, M&A activity, business expansion, headcount reduction, hiring, remote working, contracting with third parties, major contract win and the list goes on.

Other times you can trigger a conversation that leads to a compelling event and the questions before and the chapter that follows is for that purpose.

Chapter

10 Conversations

Saying what we think gives us a wider conversational range than saying what we know.

Cullen Hightower (quotation and quip writer, 1923 - 2008)

IT is almost certainly the case that you will have been party to a conversation about the cloud. The hardest question to answer is usually: can you explain to me what the cloud is in a few words?

The authors have put together ten topical conversations points about the cloud and Office 365 and one of them is our attempt to answer the question before.

Know your customer

It is a trait of the IT industry that as a progressive industry we are faced with the constant challenge of selling to customers the 'new' (what we have to sell today) while recognising the value of the 'old' (what we sold last year). As technology becomes business DNA there is a need to know your customer's business and if that is the supply of fruit and vegetables then their supply chain is uppermost. Technology can help businesses and the starting point for that is to understand what is important to your customer.

They have $25000 to allocate to a project to improve the performance of their business - why would they choose to invest that in IT? What challenges do they have in communicating and collaborating with their supply chain? Is Office 365 a solution?

Drip Drip Drip

Over time businesses have accumulated an inventory of IT and some of that is ageing. It does the job but is a niggling source of dissatisfaction and that could be associated with cost or its fitness for purpose. We are moving to a world where innovation is on a constant drip feed in the cloud and the notion of having to allocate time and resources to perform software upgrades is becoming a quaint old custom. This has implications for you if you offered those upgrade services.

What is your plan?

Break free

IT comes with cost and complexity and for a long time we assumed that is the way it has to be. The complexity has become a burden with up to 80% of IT budgets allocated to keeping the lights on. That leaves little to get creative and the channel for delivery of creativeness today is the cloud as this where developers have gravitated to reach global audiences. So to help your customers break free from the burden of the cost of complexity of IT you need an escape plan; an orderly plan as throw away is not an option for most customers. A plan that carries over their investment made in people skills and gain access to the pool of innovation in the cloud. Customers are looking for help and guidance.

Your customers are ready for this conversation. Are you?

What really matters?

Did you build the car you drive? Do you service it yourself? Unless you are highly skilled and have the necessary equipment the answer is almost certainly No. In so many areas of our life we have come to terms with the fact that it is the function that we want and not the machine. The IT industry has built the infrastructure (the machine are datacentres) and they serve up the function. Every industry goes through change and the IT industry thrives on this and your customers need you to translate this change into what it means for their business. If you don't, someone else will.

Bring out the storyteller in you. You are ready for this conversation?

IT as a utility

When, or perhaps as IT becomes a utility it is characteristic that customers will be more comfortable in a self-service mode and with computer literacy increasing the customer is en-route to becoming more self-reliant anyway. It is then incumbent on the supplier (you) to understand how to serve the increasingly self-reliant customer and deliver something of value that the customer will pay for. The Internet put a shock wave through many industries that have had to reconfigure their business model and the IT industry is now itself in a state of business transformation for that reason.

"The server room is now a meeting room and all our applications and data are in the cloud. We got rid of the hardware and software we just see IT as a utility that our provider takes care of. I think we've got all our bases covered."

How do you plan to respond?

Outcomes trump technology

When your customer bought IT assets for its business the business conversation and the technology conversation became one because of the need to understand 'what's in the box'. The cloud simplifies this conversation, the box is now a service, and keeps it focussed on the business outcomes and while that is something we are trained to do, we are often distracted by technology. Cloud services put the technology in the background and bring to the forefront the 'business outcomes'.

How might this change your sales engagement?

BYOD is the new way

Businesses used to issue IT to its employees and they would sign a chit saying they would look after it and return it when they leave. Later organisations developed policies to ensure employees understood their obligations to protect the data stored on their computers. This was also designed to evidence to the regulator (e.g. Information Commissioner's Office in the UK) that the organisation took steps to enforce its legal responsibilities. Then the cloud made many an interesting alternative available to store information and share that information with others both inside and outside the organisation. To compound this scenario and confound the IT folks desire for control this is happening on devices owned by the employee. This spawned the terms Bring YOD, now giving way to Choose YOD and for a bit of humour Grow YOD. The thing is: no one size fits all anymore. Actually if you think about it; many people are quite happy to absorb the cost of the devices (phone, tablet, computer) from personal income for personal and work use.

What opportunity does that present employers? Have you had that conversation?

Game changer

Help your customer create a list of IT that is unique to their business where unique means there is no available alternative. Why? Your customer needs to remain competitive (unless they have no competitors) and you can help them understand how they can achieve that with IT. Part of the answer is keeping the cost of IT comparable to the lowest cost your competitor would have for the same function. This is different thinking for an industry that has chosen to promote 'competitive advantage' as rationale for IT investment but time has proven that this is elusive and quickly replicated. IT is becoming utility and like other utilities you shop for the best deal. If you buy energy for your business at a cost price that is 5% higher than your competitor you would want to remedy that. IT is not fungible (yet) like electricity; it is being served up 'as a service' in the cloud with the characteristics of a utility with utility pricing. This is a game changer for customers and suppliers.

Is everyone that is customer facing ready for this conversation?

Later IT!

More and more LOB managers are using their budgets to buy IT - they want outcomes NOT technology. What does this mean for you? The cloud is an easy place to go for these LOB managers as they justify they are buying a service, not IT, and circumvent the IT department.

Where is your loyalty now?

Stealth IT

Your friends in the IT department feel some threat with this so called 'stealth IT' bought by LOB managers so how do you get them on-side as you trawl the organisation finding those LOB managers with money to spend? If you don't someone else will.

Dilemma?

And finally the authors get to answer the question at the beginning of this chapter.

The cloud is...

A utility that delivers easy and affordable access to software and content accessed via the Internet. It has many uses: for work, for learning, our social existence and for play. With technology pervasive in our lives we crave simplicity, depend on mobility, need affordability and delight at innovation and the cloud is the driving force to deliver this. It is changing how we think of and make use of computers, tablets and mobile phones.

That is a lot to remember so let us suggest this abbreviated version.

For those businesses that depend on IT, then the cloud is a better way to run a business.

We are interested in how you would write your version of: The cloud is...

Please send it to *feedback@Smart-Questions.com* and we will publish it and credit it to you (or be anonymous) on our web site.

Chapter

9

Funny you should say that

Laughter gives us distance. It allows us to step back from an event, deal with it and then move on.

Bob Newhart (Comedian, 1929 –)

CLOUD Computing sounds great in theory. We trust that the questions and ideas in the previous chapters were valuable. However you may be feeling that the book is missing some stories or anecdotes from services providers who are out there in the real world. If that is the case then this is the chapter for you.

If we'd interspersed these stories with the questions it would have made the Chapters too long. It would also have prevented you using the questions as checklists or aide-memoires. So we've grouped together our list of stories in this Chapter. I'm sure that you have your own stories – both positive and negative - so let us know them:

stories@smart-questions.com

Office 365 solves challenge of two merged businesses

With change comes opportunity

Sales often look for a compelling event and when two companies in the construction industry come together as a result of acquisition then you have that event. When each business has its own IT legacy the integration of the businesses presents a significant set of challenges and cost implications. It also is a trigger to look at new ways to deliver IT that accommodates the IT legacy and provides a platform for the future, for growth and to absorb the next acquisition. With the importance of IT its adaptability to changing business circumstances is something that has brought cloud to the attention of senior management as a way to mitigate some of the risk associated with investment in IT, after all who can see 3 to 5 years into the future?

Partner for success

Microsoft's commitment to the cloud is unswerving and its relentless promotion of cloud has influenced customers' propensity to consider cloud and IT departments are now driving this conversation. IT departments manage a large of number of supplier relationships and can make connections between suppliers that serve the business in different ways and this is fertile for Microsoft partners to increase their influence and opportunity in an account. Which suppliers have most influence, often a measure of revenue, who is the supplier for mobile communications and WAN as they support the infrastructure that deliver the connectivity for cloud services? Find out who they are or ask the IT department for introductions and broker a relationship where you look for opportunities to collaborate on projects where you bring specialist Microsoft skills and knowledge of tools like Nuix to solve technical challenges associated with data migration.

Big and complex – no worries

Two businesses merge, one with 16000 people, the other 5000, they have legacy Exchange email and 32 terabytes of archive data across two environments. The project had a number of dimensions all delivering value from the decision to deliver a cloud solution.

Complex yes, solvable yes, Office 365 definitely. Office 365 is a solution for all sizes of business and simple and complex projects and the bigger the project the more opportunity for services so we look for these opportunities to differentiate our proposition.

Mobility calls for Enterprise Mobility Services (EMS)

In an organisation of 21000 people you can bet they don't all sit at a desk all day and the construction industry is highly mobile. Providing secure access to IT from a variety of devices, often in unusual situations like the top of a building under construction, needs a solution that goes anywhere and EMS is that solution. With mobility high on the agenda of IT then EMS provides a single source solution from Microsoft and can save money compared to a number of stand-alone solutions and that is music to ears of a customer. With the need to work on any device from anywhere Office 365 is also the base to deliver web conferencing with Lync, OneDrive, SharePoint Online and the Office Suite to help people get the job done from anywhere.

Cost savings

Bringing all 32 terabytes of data from legacy EMC and HP archiving solutions together in Office 365 delivered significant cost savings in terms of licenses and management efficiencies. The reduction in datacentre load with the move to Office 365 paved the way to ultimately decommission the datacentres to deliver further savings. The migration of all users to Office 365 alone delivers a saving of £2.5M over 5 years. Those savings would not have been available without considering cloud as an alternative to building out more infrastructure on-premises.

Business prosperity

Most often prosperity is a measure of financial success but it has another measure, the output of the people that deliver that financial success. When the culture of a business is supported by technology to deliver output, often a factor of the ease that colleagues can communicate and collaborate, then that serves everyone to deliver against the core values of the business. It may sound a cliché yet the output of a disparate workforce of 21000 people can be enhanced by technology that delivers communication and collaboration on any device from anywhere, and in any event that is the way we increasingly work. That is what Office 365 delivers and the result is business prosperity.

As the provider our prosperity comes with the reward of project that has a rolling plan and a 5-year contract that is hard to achieve with the resale of hardware and software. That is the upside of helping a customer with the digital transformation of their business enabled by cloud services from Microsoft.

Dan Scarfe, Founder DotNet Solutions

http://www.dotnetsolutions.co.uk/

Office 365 connects mobile workforce in services sector

Office 365 for mobile workers

Communicating with mobile workers that are not connected to any specific place of work is common to many industries and a challenge for internal communication that relies on the distribution of paper to home addresses and posting on notice boards that is expensive and sometimes error prone. When you have 4000 mobile workers and a 24/7 business that is a lot of cost and needs a solution that is both cost-effective and have high user acceptance. Searching for a solution this customer turned to Bytes to meet the challenge of the distribution of critical information, such as updated health and safety policies, and meet its obligations as a responsible employer and serve frontline employees to deliver a great customer experience.

Access to timely information

In a fast moving environment and timetables to be met it is important that employees have access to up to-date information wherever they are. All employees use mobile phones and this provided the opportunity to use that device as the route to communicate with the employee and provide access to information without the need to impose on the employee's mobile phone preference. It was anticipated this Bring Your Own Device (BYOD) policy would support high user acceptance of Office 365, and of course save the business money, as it would not have to buy equipment. A win –win.

Office 365 delivers productivity

The sum of productivity can be measured in many ways, more in the same or less time freeing up time to spend with customers to deliver a superior customer experience. In services industries delivering a great customer experience is an indicator to repeat business and referrals and employees that are where they need to be when needed and connected with access to information can deliver more for the customer. How much productivity do you need to justify an investment in Office 365? This customer estimated a productivity gain of 3,800 hours each and every day for its 4,000 mobile workers. Add to that the dilution of the costs associated with distribution of paper and contribution to a socially responsible green agenda and you have a compelling business case.

Summing up

Mobile workers can now be easily connected from any device and from anywhere they have a connection to the Internet to work more productively. A BYOD policy speeds up the implementation of Office 365 and user acceptance. In a world where your customers are connected to email and other online services it makes sense to equip those that serve them with the same services and if they are mobile then Office 365 goes everywhere they go.

John Garidis, Bytes Cloud Practice Lead

www.bytes.co.uk

Office 365 on the radar of IT

The IT team is your ally

Sometimes the dream opportunity comes your way: selling Microsoft Office 365 to a customer you never actually met, taking an order for a 580-seat migration from Exchange, to deliver resilience and to quickly provision services for new users. Other times you have to work harder and find a route to engage a customer. In the latter circumstance, IT can be you ally says Lyndon Evans, Business Development Lead at Cloud Services Provider Outsourcery.

In this instance, the recommendation is to talk to IT to discover the backlog and who owns the business problem and ask for an introduction. Don't overlook the opportunity to work with the IT team to explore the services that they are under pressure, or under-resourced, to deliver, which could so easily be improved with a migration to Office 365. IT is strategic to business and patching servers is not strategic work.

Sell a vision, not a product

IT teams are busy maintaining IT, often with a 'keep the lights on' approach and in a mid-sized company that can be a full-time job for three or four people. This is necessary work but leaves little time for innovation. Given the vital function IT performs, these teams are connected in the organisation top to bottom, so sales teams should think about how to use those relationships to gain access to others across the business.

And whilst it is feasible that all IT can be moved to the cloud, Evans advises not to 'fork lift' everything, but rather to look for a workload that is a pain point and solve that, using Office 365, painting a vision that builds on Office 365 as a platform for the future delivery of IT.

Solve first, conquer later

Office 365 has many components that can be implemented selectively to solve a number of business requirements, such as the availability of universal content using SharePoint. Evans' experience is that this is highly relevant to fragmented or departmentalised organisations along with a whole range of teams from sales and marketing to HR and customer service functions. The 'solving' part is in explaining how SharePoint can streamline access to content. That becomes a tangible benefit when delivered 'as a service' at an economic price point that is a compelling entrée to later introduce other Office 365 components.

Evans' advice is to elevate the conversation about SharePoint, so that far from being just a 'place to store documents', it becomes 'the solution to information governance'. Position yourself as a trusted advisor and use the opportunity to demonstrate your expertise. When the inevitable reply is, "Oh we hadn't thought of SharePoint in that way... tell us more", you then have an open door to further the conversation.

Take the lead

For many customers, this is a new conversation and they will expect you to take the lead, so put their business first as you look to solve business problems, rather than simply looking to the sale. This will further position you as a trusted consultant and what's more, is a reflection of the relationships you will need to develop that comes with being the provider of IT 'as a service'. Recognise that they may have concerns and address them early in the sales cycle. Security is a known area of concern, so lead the conversation and allay any fears – some of which will be unfounded due to hearsay – and refer to reliable resources, such as Microsoft's Office 365 Trust Centre.

There are many opportunities with Office 365 and the economics of the subscription model are compelling, but as Evans concludes, "don't lead with cost". Instead, tell a story about how Office 365 is transforming the way that IT serves the business. Put simply, it is a better way.

Lyndon Evans is a Fellow of the British Computer Society and Business Development Lead at Outsourcery, the cloud experts.

Find out more at *www.outsourcery.co.uk*

Or on Twitter @Outsourcery

Office 365 fuel for visionaries

People first not IT

What is your biggest asset? Most often people are top of the list and that fits neatly into how we conduct our business with customer, people first, then move to process and technology. We look to test the chemistry between Cloudamour and our customers as we set out to search where we can make a difference and knockdown myths about what is and is not possible. A conversation that is rich in understanding the opportunity of mobile working, sharing knowledge and getting work done made easy by technology.

Once we have exposed the customer's hot buttons we propose they come to Cloudamour to see how we eat, sleep and drink cloud. Welcome to your Customer Immersion Experience, we don't speak to slides, we hold a conversation and show what is possible, to inspire, to build a vision – the big picture. Is this a vision for your business? OK, now let's talk about how we build that for your people and your business. We create the thirst before we serve the drinks. Our prize is reflected in our order book, more and bigger orders.

The T in IT is for Transformation

Moving work to the cloud raises a number of questions around access, security, data sovereignty and the opportunity to talk about what is better and not constrained by human intervention to maintain equilibrium. The new conversation shifts to focus on what people need to do a better job and transform how they communicate and collaborate to do that. Business leaders understand that the culture of an organisation can be enriched by technology when it is designed to support how people work and that includes how they share using social media. Tell it one way and it is a scary place, told another way it is the place every one imagines they want to go to work.

Get to the point quickly

A conversation about technology can quickly spiral out of control whereas a conversation that is about what is important to the customer is a good place. At Cloudamour we set the tone for a conversation by focussing on:

1. People – what's important to them and makes a difference
2. Mobile – naturally and let's ensure it is secure
3. Innovation – where things get done rather than get in the way

Building a bridge to the vision that can only be achieved with the support of people that are inspired by change and then you have to deliver.

Happy days and happy customers

Customers are migrating to the cloud and Office 365 and we will help them when we create and deliver on a vision that we deliver over time and the basis of a lasting relationship that keeps us connected with the customer in one way. In another way we are happy to be less connected with the customer as experience highlights that prior to moving to the cloud customer calls to service desk average 1.2 calls per month per user, and after moving to the cloud reduce to 0.8 calls per month per user. That is good business all round.

Safe is risky

It used to be said that 'do nothing is always an option' and that is out-dated as it leaves you exposed to those that decide that 'safe is risky'. The cloud has created a tidal wave of innovation that is affordable and keeps you at the front of the pack rather than the back and applies to Cloudamour as a Microsoft partner and the customers we serve.

Mitchell Feldman, CEO Cloudamour

https://cloudamour.com/

Office 365 takes away the pain for SMEs

SME – Small Medium and Exceptional

How does a partner new to selling Office 365 win their first customers? They start by identifying the customer segment they choose to serve and, as Tim Browne CEO of Phormium IT Solutions Ltd explains, they have the culture to serve the SME customer, typically between 10 and 250 users. Phormium is a small business and for this reason they have insight to the challenges of a small business; they can easily relate to SME owner/managers.

SME can be different

Many resellers like to build an inventory of their customers installed base and look for opportunity there. What is ageing and due an upgrade? Is all the software licensed and on the current version?

Have you checked the weather forecast for the location of your customers' business and is their business premises in an area prone to flooding? What would be the consequences for the business? One of Phormium customers is in a location prone to flooding, so what opportunity does that present?

The cost of premises is a major overhead for businesses and they move to find good rental deals, so what are the implications of 'lift and shift IT' when they move? Another of Phormium's customers had moved three times in three years, in search of keeping their premises costs low.

You plan for the worst scenario and then the worst happens: the plan wasn't fool proof. SharePoint had grown from a few documents to something that was fundamental to the day-to-day work of the business. The customer thought, or was that more of a wish, that SharePoint was being backed up. It wasn't and everything was lost. A painful lesson, never again. They turned to Phormium for advice and the solution had to be bullet proof.

The CEO of the business spent four weeks in the UK and 4 weeks in Australia; there is a ten-hour time difference. The business needs to operate like a global office even though it is a 12-person SME. They had a SBS server that was a headache to manage and going end of life. They were running out of time and needed to know their options and they had to be affordable, so they called in Phormium to deliver a future proof solution.

No dedicated IT staff

All of the business mentioned above had no IT staff. The business had staff numbers ranging from 12 to 50. Most SMEs cannot afford dedicated IT staff, yet are reliant on IT as much as businesses that have a CIO and army of IT professionals. This is ideal territory for Phormium who understand the challenges of 'surviving' IT as a SME. Once upon a time there was only one option, to buy and own and operate IT and hope it all worked. Today, SME's want to unload the burden of IT so they can focus on what they do, to earn money, and Phormium makes that happen. Tim Browne says: "We take away the hassle of IT and deliver a 'better way' for SMEs to consume IT that is affordable, accessible from anywhere, using any device, and always available when you need".

Office 365

It solves many different requirements for customers and they may not always be conventionally described as IT challenges. Look for the obvious and also ask questions to reveal what is not so obvious and since many SME owner/managers take personal responsibility for IT, take away their worries so they can focus on earning money and delighting their customers.

Tim Browne, CEO Phormium IT Solutions Ltd

http://www.phormium-it.co.uk/

Chapter

Final Word

A conclusion is the place where you got tired of thinking.

Albert Bloch (American Artist, 1882 – 1961)

AND finally we arrive at the closing summary where you wrap everything up in one simple set of words.

Only you can decide on the value of selling Office 365, it is your business, your future. We have provided in this book food for the conversation that will help you and your colleagues decide.

Others that have been down this path have resolved their decision on factors that may be different to your own. Sometimes one reason is enough, other times you need more.

- You have checked with all your customers to know if they are using cloud services and why.
- You have an inventory of all Microsoft products sold to all customers so you know who to go talk to about Office 365.
- You understand all the reasons why it is important to you to sell your customers Office 365.
- You have configured your sales and support processes with the trained resources to take Office 365 to your customers.
- You are aware of the risks of inaction and the threat of competitors' actions.

Now we hand back to you since at the end of the day, you know your business and it is your future and you make the decisions.

Appendix

CAPEX

A capital expense associated with assets such as equipment, property and buildings. This is a drain on cash or may require borrowing to finance the acquired asset. The general rule is that if the useful life of the acquired asset (e.g. a computer) is longer than the taxable year (in which it is acquired) then the cost must be capitalized. The capital expenditure costs are then depreciated over the life of the asset in question. This is typically how the cost of IT assets has been treated in the past.

Microsoft CSP program

The Microsoft Cloud Solution Provider program is a resource for partners to:

- Create a customer offer, set the price, and own the billing terms.
- Integrate service offerings with Microsoft cloud services.
- Stay at the centre of the Microsoft cloud customer lifecycle.

ENISA

The European Union agency for Network Information and Security (ENISA) is the EU's response to cyber security issues. Their statement about security and cloud computing reveals an interesting point of view that is often overlooked.

'Put simply, all kinds of security measures are cheaper when implemented on a larger scale. Therefore the same amount of investment in security buys better protection. This includes all kinds of defensive measures such as filtering, patch management, hardening of virtual machine instances and hypervisors, human resources and their management and vetting, hardware and software redundancy, strong authentication, efficient role-based access control and federated identity management solutions by default, which also improves the network effects of collaboration among various partners involved in defense (sic).'

NIST definition of cloud computing

The most referenced definition of cloud computing from the National Institute of Science and Technology (NIST).

NIST's definition lists five essential characteristics of cloud computing: on-demand self-service, broad network access, resource pooling, rapid elasticity or expansion, and measured service.

It also lists three 'service models' (software (SaaS), platform (PaaS) and infrastructure (IaaS)), and four 'deployment models' (private, community, public and hybrid) that together categorise ways to deliver cloud services.

The definition is intended to serve as a means for broad comparisons of cloud services and deployment strategies, and to provide a baseline for discussion from what is cloud computing to how to best use cloud computing.

OPEX

An operating expense associated with the on-going cost for running a product, business or system ('running costs'). Many cloud services are available under term agreements with a defined payment schedule (e.g. monthly) and these payments to the cloud services provider are treated as OPEX. For some businesses this is kinder on cash flow and as cash is the lifeline of business this is an attractive choice.

On-premises

The IT assets of a business are located on-premises owned by the business. Many consider this is the way to control the physical security of and access to these assets. In truth all businesses fall well short of being able to provide the level of security needed to protect these assets when compared to Microsoft. For a statement supporting this point of view please refer above to ENISA.

Own and Operate

A term used to describe the operational mode of a business that chooses to own their IT assets and employ people to operate and maintain those assets. In a 24x7 world this is no small undertaking and IT has been a significant cost and a focus for efficiency. There are alternatives now so the default for most businesses is to compare own and operate versus 'as a service' available from Microsoft and its partners.

Net Present Value (NPV)

Since IT is such a significant cost to most businesses it has a big financial implication and when a customer is considering a new investment they may want (you) to calculate the NPV for that investment. Fortunately there is a function in Excel to help you perform this calculation.

Net present value (NPV) or net present worth (NPW) is defined as the sum of the present values (PVs) of incoming and outgoing cash flows over a period of time. Incoming and outgoing cash flows can also be described as benefit and cost cash flows, respectively.

Subscription

Used to describe a variable term commitment to a service; day(s), month(s), year(s). Look carefully at your options to exit and stop paying for the service. Office 365 is offered on subscription terms with monthly and annual billing options to suit the customer.

Total Cost of Ownership (TCO)

You may be asked to compare the TCO of an on-premises solution with the same function in the cloud.

TCO is the purchase price of an asset plus the costs of operation over a given time period (typically 3 to 5 years). The option with the lower total cost of ownership will be the better value in the long run.

Bibliography & Links

URLs correct at time of publication

Microsoft Cloud Solution Provider (CSP) program

https://mspartner.microsoft.com/en/us/pages/solutions/cloud-reseller-overview.aspx

How to Win Friends and Influence People by Dale Carnegie

http://en.wikipedia.org/wiki/Dale_Carnegie

Escape Velocity by Geoffrey Moore

http://www.escapevelocitybymoore.com/

The Challenger Sale by Matthew Dixon and Brett Adamson

http://www.executiveboard.com/exbd/sales-service/challenger-sale/index.page

Thinking of…Selling Microsoft Office 365? Ask the Smart Questions by Frank Bennett, Dan Lewis and Stephen Parker. Available to download from MPN

https://mspartner.microsoft.com

NIST definition of Cloud Computing

http://csrc.nist.gov/publications/nistpubs/800-145/SP800-145.pdf

European businesses face a tech deficit

http://www.colt.net/uk/en/news/72-of-european-businesses-face-a-tech-deficit-en.htm

UK IT Directors on end-user computing strategy as an enabler of business innovation.

http://www.information-age.com/technology/cloud-and-virtualisation/123458410/readjusting-view-end-user-computing-rise-do-it-yourself-it

IDC forecast for SaaS

http://www.idc.com/getdoc.jsp?containerId=249834

Gartner forecast for cloud office systems

http://www.gartner.com/newsroom/id/2514915

Gartner 'Nexus of Forces'

http://www.gartner.com/technology/research/nexus-of-forces/

IDC 'The Third Platform'

http://www.idc.com/

ENISA

http://www.enisa.europa.eu/

Getting Involved

The Smart Questions community

There may be questions that we should have asked but didn't. Or specific questions which may be relevant to your situation, but not everyone in general. Go to the website for the book and post the questions. You never know, they may make it into the next edition of the book. That is a key part of the Smart Questions Philosophy.

Send us your feedback

We love feedback. We prefer great reviews, but we'll accept anything that helps take the ideas further and welcome your comments on this book.

We'd prefer email, as it's easy to answer and saves trees. If the ideas worked for you, we'd love to hear your success stories. Maybe we could turn them into 'Talking Heads'-style video or audio interviews on our website, so others can learn from you. That's one of the reasons why we wrote this book. So talk to us.

feedback@smart-questions.com

Got a book you need to write?

Maybe you are a domain expert with knowledge locked up inside you. You'd love to share it and there are people out there desperate for your insights. But you don't think you are an author and don't know where to start. Making it easy for you to write a book is part of the Smart Questions Philosophy.

Let us know about your book idea, and let's see if we can help you get your name in print.

potentialauthor@Smart-Questions.com

Notes pages

We hope that this book has inspired you and that you have already scribbled your thoughts all over it. However if you have ideas that need a little more space then please use these notes pages.

www.ingramcontent.com/pod-product-compliance
Lightning Source LLC
LaVergne TN
LVHW012333060326
832902LV00011B/1868

* 9 7 8 1 9 0 7 4 5 3 1 8 2 *